C000133164

IMAGES OF ENGLAND

THE
BANDS
PLAY ON!

IMAGES OF ENGLAND

THE
BANDS
PLAY ON!

ERIC JOHNSON

EDITED BY DAVID KENNEDY

TEMPUS

This book is a result of over ten years of research by Eric Johnson and includes the input of many local people and organisations. During the latter part of 2002 Eric became very ill. However, despite his illness, he was determined to complete this book and, only a few days before he died, he received the good news that a publisher had been found who was willing to print it.

The family wishes to thank David Kennedy for his generosity in editing the script and Glenys Cooper of Ottakar's for her persistence and enthusiasm in her quest to realise Eric's dream.

Noreen, Richard and Graham Johnson

Frontispiece: Eric Johnson and his beloved euphonium.

First published 2003

Tempus Publishing Limited
The Mill, Brimscombe Port,
Stroud, Gloucestershire, GL5 2QG

© Eric Johnson, 2003

The right of Eric Johnson to be identified as the Author of this work has been asserted in accordance with the Copyrights, Designs and Patents Act 1988.

All rights reserved. No part of this book may be reprinted or reproduced or utilised in any form or by any electronic, mechanical or other means, now known or hereafter invented, including photocopying and recording, or in any information storage or retrieval system, without the permission in writing from the Publishers.

British Library Cataloguing in Publication Data.
A catalogue record for this book is available from the British Library.

ISBN 0 7524 3079 3

Typesetting and origination by Tempus Publishing Limited
Printed in Great Britain by Midway Colour Print, Wiltshire

Contents

A euphonium rehearsal.

Editor's Note

I was most fortunate to spend precious times with this great musician, Eric Johnson. We talked of music and people, never one without the other, and always with humour and understanding. I have tried in these pages to reproduce Eric's words and his heart.

Please forgive any misjudgements I have made. I tried my best. I daresay he would have liked that.

David Kennedy, June 2003

Note

Every effort has been made to re-check copyright of photographs in this book. Thanks go to the *Burton Mail* and the *Lichfield* publications for giving permission to reproduce photographs where copyright may be held by them.

Foreword

Come listen to the band. To what paths of pleasure were these words the gateway in those halcyon days when warm Sunday evenings could be spent sitting around the bandstand in Stapenhill Recreation Grounds; or when smartly uniformed musicians marched in well-drilled formation in contests at events like Horninglow Flower Show!

Nowadays music is more likely to come from a synthesiser or heavily compiled recording equipment. The good old bands needed no loudspeakers.

Still, however, the tradition of the brass bands and kindred ensembles are being kept alive. People like Eric Johnson, much of whose working life was spent teaching young people in the schools of this district to play and enjoy playing music, can take much of the credit.

As well as travelling around the local schools, Eric ran the Burton Music Centre in Bond Street, where the young members of Burton Music Centre Brass rehearsed. They performed locally and further afield, sometimes abroad where they met and befriended young musicians of other nations.

Some of Eric's own playing was with the local Territorial Army Band but he became best known as a music teacher and as the director of several brass bands including Ind Coope, Newhall and Uttoxeter.

Sometimes those he taught as youngsters followed him from one band to another; others found bands in other areas to which their day jobs took them; some are passing on to others skills he taught them.

Added to his other achievements, Eric decided he would like to compile this book, paying tribute to local bands past and present. He dedicated many hours to research and talked to large numbers of musicians and music-lovers, over the last few years. Always there seemed to be more to find out and he went on digging for facts and pictures.

In the last few months, illness turned this labour of love into a burden, but one he gladly shouldered, so keen was he to complete and publish.

This book will stand not only as a memorial to the bands and musicians of the past and the present, but as a reminder of Eric – musician, teacher, organiser, historian and, to so many of us, a hell of a nice guy and valued friend.

Dave Stacey

Introduction

I first thought about delving into Burton Brass Band history when the *Burton Daily Mail* reprinted the *Burton Chronicle* dated 4 April 1889. This particular issue was the one predominantly dedicated to the opening of the Ferry Bridge by Lady Burton. At the banquet that followed in St Paul's Institute, the Burton Band, under the direction of Mr W. Twells, played a programme of music that included the overture *Zampa* by Herold and *The Yeoman of the Guard* by Sullivan amongst other items not now available.

Reading further into the paper, I saw an advert which read, 'Burton Robin Hood Brass Band – open to engagements. Terms (moderate) on application to the bandmaster, Mr W. Daniels, 26 Moor Street.' These items about bands in Burton caused me to wonder just how many bands had operated in the area during the past one hundred years or so.

The earliest recorded brass band (where all the instruments were indeed brass – not brass and reed) is in 1832 at an ironworks in Blaina (Monmouthshire). The following year two members of the York Waits Band formed a brass band of twenty-four players. Two of our most famous bands, Besses o' the Band and Black Dyke Mills Band, were formed in 1835 and 1837 respectively, but there are records of bands dating back to 1818, when valves were invented, which of course made playing much easier and the sound much better. Adolphe Sax developed the Saxhorn and larger brass around the same time, thus adding a completely new range of brass instruments to the trumpets and trombones.

Bearing in mind these facts, one can therefore assume that there have been brass bands in and around Burton since possibly 1840. My aim is to record whatever I can for posterity, especially in view of the remarkable increase of interest in the sound of brass today.

Eric Johnson

Above: Eric Johnson, 1990.

one

The Old Timers, 1834-1950

The following bands were first known to be in existence on the dates shown:

Woodville United Silver Prize Band	1834
Robin Hood Band	1880s
Burton Silver Prize Band	1897
Hilton and Marston-on-Dove Band	1890s
Stapenhill Band	1900
Yoxall Band	1904
Burton Excelsior Silver Band	1905
Coton Silver Prize Band	1920
Hugglescote and Ellistown Silver Prize Band	1920
Unknown (Worthington's) Band	1920s
Tutbury Silver Prize Band (Reformed)	1926
Swadlincote Band	1928
Derby Borough Police Band	1930
The Auxiliary Fire Service Band, (Burton)	1940
The Home Guard Band, (Burton)	1943
Burton Air Training Corps Band	1940s
Ind Coope and Allsopp Silver Band	1940s
Rocester Band	1950

Woodville Brass Band or Woodville United Silver Prize Band

The earliest recorded brass band in the neighbourhood was the Woodville Brass Band, founded in 1834. It began as the Wooden Box Band with the nickname of the 'Doodles Band'. No doubt it had a queer assortment of instruments compared to today's brass bands. For instance, the use of valves in instruments had only recently changed the instrumentation of bands. No doubt a number of keyed bugles, ophicleides, sackbuts and serpents were still in use along with slide trumpets – a smaller version of the slide trombone.

By 1882 the Woodville Band was known as the Woodville Orchestral Band. In 1905 the now Woodville United Silver Band could add the word 'Prize' to its title, having won the Elkington, Hazelhurst and Gisborne Challenge Cup.

Until the early 1980s, the present Woodville Working Men's Club had the sign 'Woodville Band Club' over its frontage. Unfortunately, all the records which might have shed some light on the band's history, have vanished with the refurbishment and changeover of the club.

The Woodville (John Knowles) Band of the mid-1920s. Left to right, back row: Albert Walker, John Hill, Angus Holmes, Reg Hill, -?-, Bill Fullerone. Second row: Cyril Walton, Jack Parker, Edgar Shears, Harry Smith, -?-, Fred Olsey. Front row: Arthur Blakely, Bill Blakely, Jack Boddice, Jack Hassall, John Knowles, Jack Parker Snr, William Pickford, Reginald Pickford.

Burton Silver Prize Band

Harry Reynolds formed the Burton Silver Prize Band in about 1897. They were not alone, as other local bands at that time included the Burton Salvation Army, the Salem Baptist, the Robin Hood and the Burton Band conducted by Mr W. Twells.

The Burton Silver Prize Band ventured into brass band contesting in 1907 at Tamworth Castle. In 1908 it competed at the Crystal Palace Bandsmen's Festival, London. In 1912 the band took sixth prize at the Derby Festival, and first prizes at Moira in 1913 and 1914. Most notable of all, the band gained second prize at the Crystal Palace in the Preliminary Shield Section.

After the First World War, surviving members of the band regrouped, playing their first post-war public performance at Burton Town Hall in 1920. In 1921 the band was awarded sixth prize (third section) at the Crystal Palace and, in 1923, fourth prize (second section).

Burton Silver Prize Band competed in 1923 at the Crystal Palace in a line-up of twenty-seven bands from all over Britain. They all played the overture *Ruy Blas* by Mendelssohn. The adjudicators wrote, 'A good toned band, technically capable with solid tone, clean execution and good interpretation.'

By 1921 the band was regularly playing for dances at Burton Town Hall, delighting audiences and dancers alike. A *Burton Daily Mail* report of October 1921 wrote: 'How admirably this talented combination of Burton musicians adapted to the exacting requirements of terpsichorean music.'

Possibly the greatest moment in the band's history occurred at 6.20 p.m. on a Monday evening in May 1935 when the band broadcast a programme on BBC Radio. The *Radio Times* printed the programme as follows: 'A number of letters of congratulations were printed in the *Burton Mail*, one of which said, "Until I heard this Band, I did not realize that Burton had such an excellent musical combination."'

In 1931, the band once again competed successfully at the Crystal Palace.

The outbreak of the Second World War finally silenced the band, although a few older players remained and 'had a blow', under Harry Reynolds' leadership, throughout hostilities and even afterwards for a short time.

Burton Silver Band before 1914.

Burton Silver Prize Band, 1914. A number of the bandsmen failed to return after the war, including Messrs V. Chandler, A. Slater and J. Wheeldon.

Burton Silver Prize Band on Burton's workhouse steps, 1926.

Burton Silver Prize Band, 1930–1932. Left to right, back row: D. Hughes, A. Bannister, N. Malachek, J. Reynolds, E. Clough, J. Flatt, J. Sibson, D. Marsland, R. Earp. Middle row: W. Good, G. Stretton, J. Owen, W. Sutton, H. Reynolds (conductor), C. Lunn, J. Tainton, H. Webster. Front row: G. Swan, W. Drinkwater, F. Roulstone, H. Carter, E. Prince, H. Clough, T. Silver, A. Felstead. On floor: E. Fern and A. Woodward.

Above: Burton Silver Prize Band, 1933.

Above: The National Band Festival Programme.

THE BURTON
SILVER PRIZE BAND
Conductor, H. A. Reynolds

March, Punchinello................*Rimmer*
Overture, Light Cavalry............*Suppé*
Cornet Duet, Playmates....*Greenwood*
(Soloists, S. PARKER and
H. GALLIMORE)

Two Contrasts:
In the Twilight..................*Rimmer*
The Harvesters' Country Dance
Cope
Selection, The Gondoliers....*Sullivan*
The Piper's Wedding
Kennedy Thayne
Martial Moments.....................*Winter*

POPULARITY OF THE
BRASS BAND

THAT all previous records have been broken in the entry for this Festival of 1931, in an unprecedented period of national crisis, unemployment and a general tightening of the belts of the working classes, from which these Bands are formed, is in itself the most convincing proof of the popularity of the Brass Band movement, and provides a startling phenomenon for the uninitiated, who may be excused for drawing erroneous conclusions as to the real prosperity of the people. It is, however, only another proof of the adage " That man does not live by bread alone."

Above left: The Broadcast Programme, BBC Radio, 1939.

Left: Excerpts from the National Band Festival Programme, 1931.

Burton Excelsior Silver Band

'Cox's Orange Pippins' or 'Cox's Banana Band' were two of the nicknames given to the Burton Excelsior Silver Band, which was formed in 1905 by Ernie S. Cox, a fruiterer of Uxbridge Street (97), Burton. The band rehearsed in the Robin Hood Inn, which was situated next to Briggs Engineering (now the site of the Octagon Centre). As the Robin Hood Band of the 1880s was based here, it is possible that this new band developed from players of that band under the new name and new direction.

The band's uniform was very dark green with contrasting green piping on trousers, tunic and cap. My informant, Mr John Cox of Alexandra Road, tells me that his grandfather, Ernie, conducted the band until the mid-1930s when he handed over the baton to Fred Adams who was employed as a driver for Cox's Fruit Shop.

Fred continued as bandmaster until the outbreak of the Second World War, when the band was disbanded and those players not called up for war service, plus other local bandsmen, formed the National Fire Service Band. Fred later formed the Air Training Corps Band of which I was a member for a short while.

Top: Burton Excelsior Band, *c.*1910.

Above: The Excelsior Band in New Street bus park, *c.*1930. Conductor: Ernest Cox.

Left: Fred Arnold (the author's grandfather) in the original Excelsior uniform before 1930.

The secretary of that first Excelsior Band was Ernie Cox's brother-in-law, Walter Tipper. His daughter, Mrs Gadsby, can remember the band playing regularly at Burton Town's home games on the 'Crescent' football ground, often marching from the Rifleman Inn in Derby Street, where rehearsals were held for a number of years between the wars.

Mrs Tilley of 8 Shelley Road, Swadlincote, provided me with my first photograph of the Excelsior Band, which was taken in the early 1930s and includes many well-known banding names such as Lance Booth, Ted and George Machin, Bill Cheshire, George Stretton and my grandfather, Fred Arnold. Mrs Tilley also supplied the photograph of the Crystal Palace where the Excelsior played in contest on quite a number of occasions. It was indeed a great tragedy when it was destroyed by fire on 30 November 1936. The band's most successful visit to the Crystal Palace resulted in a second prize, an excellent achievement against bands from all over the country.

Burton Excelsior Band, 1937.

The ill-fated Crystal Palace, which burnt down on 30 November 1936.

Amongst other contests was the one held at Derby on 22 August 1912, when they were placed seventh behind Burton Silver Prize (sixth), and one organised by the old *Daily Herald* newspaper (who later sponsored the National Finals at the Royal Albert Hall). This was held at Skegness and involved thirty bands (test piece: *March of the Heralds*).

A well-known saying of Ernie Cox was that when the band was in marching order, the front row was worth £500. As most of the instruments were bought by him with profits from his business, he was in a position to assess their value. He also transported the band to engagements on the back of his delivery lorry.

The First World War involved the band in many ways. Early on they led the march of new recruits from the drill hall to the railway station every Monday morning, gave many concerts in aid of war funds and, towards the end, were very much involved in the efforts to welcome back prisoners of war to Burton.

Lily Thomas's book, *Memories Grave and Gay*, written following the 1914–1918 war, praises the work of both the Burton Silver and Excelsior Bands, but she states:

> *for prolonged and enthusiastic support, we must give a palm to the Excelsior Band. They gave us two concerts, and then followed on with a parade of the town, occupying five Sundays. Not only did this put us firmly on our feet in the days of our infancy, bringing in the handsome sum of £110 13s 2d, but they introduced us to every inhabitant of the town, so that thereafter no one could plead ignorance of the existence of the work.*

She went on:

> *As in the case of the railwaymen, the Excelsior Band and their genial bandmaster, Mr E.S. Cox, offered us assistance 'for the duration'. Unfortunately, the stress of the times prevented the men from having any spare time at all – overtime was the order of the day and the men simply could not get free for a weekday performance. They offered us Sunday Sacred Concerts, as often as we required, but now there was a Watch Committee whose permission had to be obtained. Mr Cox sought this most solicitously, but such a thing could not be! In spite of the desire of the Burgesses to have this means of presenting their donations, the Watch Committee resolved to save the souls of the people in spite of themselves, and would neither consent to a street collection, a concert in the recreation grounds or the opening of a place of amusement on the Sabbath, although I was granted the free loan, without expense, of the Opera House (now the Odeon, Guild Street) for a Sunday concert. Well, well! After all, it is nice to be taken such care of!*

The Excelsior did manage to help in many ways, giving their services free for dances in aid of the fund and also assisted at the final function. The Boy Scouts and Violas Concert Party also helped considerably.

The closing dance, on 30 January 1919, at which the band supplied the music, went on until the early hours of the morning and the band, along with that of the Discharged Soldiers Federation, led the parade of prisoners of war, who marched four abreast and were marshalled by Sergeant Holmes from the Market Place to the Town Hall.

Other events of note included the all-day event at the school of St Mary and St Ann at Abbotts Bromley on the occasion of King George V's Silver Jubilee in 1935, which culminated with a giant fireworks display. The celebrating on Marstons Sports Ground on the Coronation of King George VI and Queen Elizabeth in 1937, and playing on a radio broadcast from Broad Street, Birmingham, in 1937: the Excelsior was the first local band to do so.

The band's final rehearsal was held at the Corporation Arms in New Street.

Coton in the Elms Brass Band or Coton Silver Prize Band

For such a small village, Coton really had a band of which to be proud. Their early beginnings are thought to have been just prior to the First World War, while the earliest photograph I have managed to acquire is dated around 1920.

The Coates family have been predominant since its formation, with Harold Coates as bandmaster for much of the time. In the photographs there are seven Coates, including Harold, his three brothers and their sons.

The photograph below includes Bill Wagstaff, who regularly walked with Reg Coates and his Uncle Alf from Coton to Burton on Sunday mornings in order to play with the Burton Excelsior Band.

Following the band's successes in contests at Leicester and Belle Vue, the name was changed from Coton in the Elms Brass Band to Coton Silver Prize Band.

The many activities in which the band were involved, apart from contesting, included garden parties at surrounding villages such as Rosliston, Netherseal and Clifton Campville, participating at the Alrewas and Kings Bromley shows, and playing at the bandstands at Tamworth Castle and Stapenhill Gardens.

The Second World War saw the break-up of the band, while the appeal of dance bands also added to the problems of maintaining a full band. However, Les Coates went on to form the Burton Big Band, with his wife Beryl as vocalist. It was indeed a sad loss to local music when Les died, but the band lives on to this day.

At the outbreak of the Second World War a number of players, mainly over military age from bands around Burton, formed the Home Guard Band. Harold Coates was one of these and he composed the music entitled *The Second Line*, with words by Fred Dale, which was the marching song of the Home Guard.

An early photograph of the Coton Band.

Coton in the Elms Brass Band. Left to right, back row: A Mottram, S. Foley, W. Taylor, A. Coates. Middle Row: A. Taylor, W. Fletcher, R. Coates, A. Wileman, T. Cox, E. Fern, F. Imber, E. Sco. Front row: Harold Coates (bandmaster), W. Johnson, G. Coates, S. Kinson, C. Yates, A. Mottram, E. Coates. Seated: L. Coates, H. Hubert and G. Coates.

Left: Reg and George Coates. *Right:* From left, back row: Alty Coates, –?–, Albert Mottram, S. Taylor. Front row: G. Coates, Les Coates, Arthur Mottram. Seated: Tom Durrant.

Tutbury Silver Band

The village of Tutbury had a brass band in the 1920s, according to Mr Frank Wilson, a retired schoolteacher whose father recounted numerous stories of that era, one of which was the fact that the band was called Tutbury Town Silver Prize Band. The use of the word 'Town' was due to the fact that Tutbury was classified as a town because a weekly market was held there, and 'Prize' was added to the title following the band's successes in contests, amongst which was at least one trophy won at the famous Crystal Palace Band Contests.

I know little about this band, but one story concerns cornet player Jack Cox. Jack used to take his cornet everywhere, and, on one occasion, he was a passenger in a pony trap (the most popular form of transport in those days) when somehow the trap ended upside down in a ditch. Jack's mother heard about the accident and her first remark was 'I hope he hasn't damaged his cornet.'

The band was recommenced after the First World War under the baton of Wallace Young. Mr Wilson used to listen to the band in rehearsal on Wednesday and Friday evenings, and he recalls how he and a lad named Compson were invited to learn an instrument by Mr Young. After five months of practice, they joined the band and he remembers how proud they felt when Mr Charles Parrick, a draper and outfitter who, very usefully was also the band president, measured them for their uniforms. The uniform was mid-blue with a silver stripe down each trouser leg, and a tunic with brass buttons and a blue peak cap. The bandmaster's cap had gold braid on the peak, 'scrambled egg we called it' wrote Frank Wilson.

The people of Tutbury, who each received a leaflet entitled 'Band or no Band', in which they were asked to contribute to the uniform fund, paid for the uniforms. Tutbury responded, and the uniforms were bought and first worn on Remembrance Sunday in a march from the school in Cornmill Lane to the church via High Street, Duke Street and Castle Street to the Castle Gates.

[For further detailed information about Tutbury Band please read Tutbury Variations *by the editor, David Kennedy.]*

Tutbury Band at Tutbury Castle, 1935.

Burton Air Training Corps Band at Villa Park, 1944.

The Burton Air Training Corps Band (351 Squadron)

During the last war, Fred Adams, a well-known local cornet player and dance band trumpeter, managed to obtain some of the disused brass instruments from the now defunct local bands whose members had been called up for military service. Fred set about teaching young ATC lads to play and, in a very short while, with the help of a small number of the Salvation Army Youth Band and his own two sons, he had a very good young band which performed on a good many engagements that would normally have been carried out by the senior bands.

One event of note was the playing at Villa Park for a wartime football match between England and Scotland. Another great experience was playing in numerous victory parades, in particular the 1946 parade in Birmingham.

The band also performed regularly in the now long-gone bandstands in Stapenhill Gardens and Outwoods Park.

The biggest problem of running such a band was the fact that most of the players were called up for military service when they were old enough, so there was a continuous process of teaching new players.

The Rest of the Old Timers

We cannot leave this section without mentioning some of the remaining bands in the area up to the end of the 1940s (seen in the following pictures). Though most of these bands folded after 1946, many of their players went on to join bands that survived this dark period in our history. They may be called 'The Survivors'.

Above and below: Hilton and Marston Brass Band.

Above: Stapenhill Band, *c.*1900. (Photograph from Mrs Holdcroft)

Below: Hugglescote and Ellistown Silver Prize, *c.*1920. (Photograph from Jack Wilkinson)

Derby Borough Police Band.

Rolls Royce Band. (Photograph from Mrs Smith)

Opposite, above: Swadlincote Band, *c.*1928.

Opposite, below: The band, *c.*1930.

The Auxiliary Fire Service Band (Burton), 1940.

Ind Coope and Allsop Silver Band, *c.*1950.

Rocester Band, *c.*1950.

two

The Survivors

The following bands were first known to be in existence on the dates shown:

Newhall Band	1850(?)
Gresley Old Hall Band	1850
Burton Salvation Army Band	1886
Swadlincote Salvation Army Band	1935
Burton Citadel Young People's Band	1950s
Ind Coope and Allsopp Silver Band	1950

The Newhall Band

The origins of the Newhall Band go back to before the turn of the century, but details are rather sketchy about how and why it was formed. However, nearby Woodville had a band in the mid-1830s and by 1900 were entering contests, so it is fairly reasonable to assume that Newhall were not far behind in forming a band, as were Gresley and Swadlincote.

The Newhall Band was a very useful village band, and by 1935 was good enough to be auditioned for a broadcast on the BBC, which went out on 17 June 1935.

Newhall St John's Band, 1905. Prior to this band were Newhall Excelsior Band and Newhall Celebration Band, c.1890.

Newhall Band before broadcasting for the first time in 1935. Left to right, back row: Ben Wardle, Spug Parker, Eric Sharpe, Norman Harvey, Fred Webster, Rob Meddings, Charlie Draycott. Middle row: Jimmy Attwood, Gearge Poulson, George Dawson, Cyril Smith, Bill Smith, Henty Wapples, Jack Greaves, Cyril Horobin. Front row: Dick Webster, George Webster, Tommy Draycott, Walter Staley, George Watson, Jimmy Sibson, (B.M.) Charley Starkey, Billy Draycott, Tommy Taylor, George Greaves.

Newhall Band in the early 1950s. Band Master: Digger Draycott.

Newhall Band, *c*.1960, with conductor Harry Doughty.

Burton Constructional Newhall Band, *c*.1974, with M.D. Ernest Woodhouse.

A new conductor, Ernest Woodhouse, took over the band in 1969; he had previously conducted a number of top bands in the Midlands but now accepted the challenge of steering Newhall to the top flight. Sponsorship was considered, and the Burton Constructional Engineering firm became the band's first sponsors. A few years later, the greetings card giants Webb Ivory of Burton became the new sponsors, with the firm's president, Mr Frank Kerry, becoming the band's president and Mr Archie Gentles taking a very great interest in the band.

By now the band was well established in the top flight. In 1978 the band swept the board at the Milton Keynes Festival and also at Basingstoke's Lansing Bagnall Festival. Later in the year they came in the top three at the Midlands area contest at Leicester's De Montfort Hall, which enabled them to appear in the National Finals at the Royal Albert Hall in October, a really great occasion.

The fame of the band and the excellence of its playing brought about recordings, including one with the well known John Inman of *Are You Being Served?* fame, and also a number of broadcasts on national radio, including two with Charlie Chester, two on Radio Three and one on a programme called *With Brass and Strings*.

Right: Webb Ivory Newhall Band rehearsing for a broadcast with musical director, Ernest Woodhouse.

Below: Webb Ivory Newhall Band with guest conductor Harry Mortimer OBE. The band was also the John Player Band of the Year.

1975. Left to right: Alan Brooks, Arthur Day, Johnny Cresswell, Eric Johnson.

Left to right: Bill Hardy, Robin Mansfield, Ralph Blakett.

Arthur Bailey and Betty Swingler.

Left to right: Jack Inger, John Beresford, Howard Smith, Martin Booth.

The band's third radio appearance, in July 1978, lasted about forty-five minutes and included a tenor horn solo by Ralph Blackett, a post horn solo by my son, Graham Johnson, and a euphonium solo by myself.

A tour of Holland and Belgium was next on the list where, in addition to giving numerous public performances, they also broadcast from Radio Hilversum. The band also played at the Airborne Forces Cemetery at Oosterbeck near Arnhem, where a wreath was laid in memory of the British troops who lost their lives in the Battle of Arnhem.

The Newhall Band covered 1,500 miles in seven days on their tour and played five concerts. They were met with enthusiasm everywhere. Typical of the reception they received was the reaction of the audience at Lent, Belgium, where the crowd refused to allow them to leave the stage. Band chairman, Harold Hardman, said: 'I simply lost count of how many encores we played that night.'

Since Mr Woodhouse's retirement in the early eighties, a succession of conductors has maintained the Newhall Band as a hard-working local band, and a great deal of gratitude for this must go to the principle cornetist, Peter Woodings, and the late Arthur Murphin, for many years the band's secretary, whose unstinting devotion to the Newhall Band must surely be recognised.

Recently, the band engaged a new musical director, Mr Mark Phillips, who brings with him a wealth of experience from several of this country's top bands. Appointed in early January 2001, he took the band to the Midlands Region Qualifying Contest in March 2001.

Webb Ivory Newhall Band at Burton Town Hall. Conductor: Ernest Woodhouse.

The Prominent Fluid Controls Newhall Band, 1988. The Newhall Band, under their new sponsorship, are pictured here at the Isle of Man contest.

Newhall Band, 1993, with musical director Eric Johnson.

Newhall Band, 1999.

Gresley Old Hall Band History

A band was first in existence here around 1850 and was known as the Gresley Band. The first recorded mention of the band was in the *Burton Weekly News* of 21 July 1857, where it was stated that the Gresley Band played at the Newhall Horticultural Exhibition.

The band underwent several name changes over the years. Possibly the first was Gresley Silver Prize Band, most likely as a result of winning a prize at a contest. It also became known as Gresley Ambulance Band, then Church Gresley Colliery Band, after which it became South Derbyshire Miners Welfare Band and finally Gresley Old Hall Band, which it remains as to this day.

When the band was associated with the colliery ambulance service, rehearsals used to be held in the ambulance station, which necessitated moving two of the ambulances out before the band could get in. It was not unusual for an injured miner to be taken to hospital to the strains of *Colonel Bogey*.

Gresley Colliery Silver Prize Band, *c*.1925. From left, back row: A. Harper, J. Roulstone,
H. Broster, S. Graves. Second row: J. Parker, C. Shepperd, W. Woollett, Y. Broster, H. Mawby,
J. Sibson, A. Harper, G. Cooper, J. Hodgkins. Third row: A. Wileman, F. Eames, C. Woollett,
J. Ife, S. Bosworth, W. Fancourt, L. Boddice, H. Martin, W. Fletcher. Fourth row: G. Webster,
W. Watson, J. Simkins, J. Smithard, W. Wileman (bandmaster), A.E. Bramley, W. Ward,
W. Parker, I. Curtis, J. Bannister.

The annual St John's Ambulance Parade, Skegness.

With the introduction of Nationalisation in 1947, the band carried on as before but moved to The Miners Arms for their rehearsals. When the Gresley Colliery closed in 1968, the band moved to its present headquarters at Gresley Old Hall and changed its name to the South Derbyshire Miners' Welfare Band. With the eventual closure of all the local pits, the name became the Gresley Old Hall Band.

In its time the band has had many conductors. In the early days they included the following: Mr L. Boddice; Mr H. Broster; Mr G. Fancourt; Mr A. Lunn; Mr H. Middleton; Mr Massey and Mr E. Johnson. In the late seventies, Warrant Officer Peter Hannan was appointed. He went on to be promoted to Lieutenant Colonel in charge of the Guards Bands and was awarded the MBE. Mr D. Blakeson, Mr Ron Banks, Mr Ray Stuttard, Mr R. Birch, Mr Howard Smith, Mr Alan Tyler and the present conductor, Mr David Hutchinson, followed him.

From the mid-seventies the band had considerable success with contesting, including the National Finals on two occasions, gaining promotion to section two and beating local rivals Newhall and Ind Coope at the Burton Festival. The band gained a fifth place at Pontin's in a contest of twenty-three bands, won the Coal Industry Championships at Blackpool and was first in the North East Midlands contest, a qualifier for the National Championships at the Symphony Hall in Birmingham.

The Gresley Band's most famous son, Nigel Boddice, often returns to his roots after twenty years as principle trumpet with the Scottish Symphony Orchestra and as conductor of the finest youth band in Scotland, the West Lothian Youth Band. He is presently conductor of a Norwegian brass band. The Gresley Band is always in big demand locally and now has a junior band to ensure the its future.

At the Brass Band Regional Championships (Midland area) in March 2003 the band was placed third in the first section – entitling them to compete in the Brass Band National Finals in Dundee.

The marriage of Susan Bellamy (tenor horn) and John Beresford (bass trombone), both with the South Derbyshire Miners Welfare Band.

Above: South Derbyshire Miners Welfare Band. Conductor: A. Lunn.

Below: South Derbyshire Miners Welfare Band, *c.*1968.

South Derbyshire Miners Welfare Band outside Blackpool Opera House, 1970s.

Gresley Old Hall Band, 2003. (Photograph from Steve Kirk)

Burton Salvation Army Band

Formed in 1886, the Burton Salvation Army Band moved into the Burton Citadel when it opened in 1889.

Burton Citadel Band. Band Leader: T. Hussey, *c*.1910.

The band in 'new' band caps instead of the white military helmets, *c*.1890.

The Salvation Army Band, *c.*1900.

The growing 'Army' Band of the 1920s. Bandmaster: P. Borley. From left, back row: C. Matkin, C. Teat, W. Hathaway, –?–, –?–, ? Grantham, W. Forrester, H. Williams, W. Matkin. Second row: W. Smedley, H. Sales, ? Warne, H. Simnet, W. Porter, –?– , W. Driver, G. Toon. Third row: H. Copeland, W. Kirkland, H. Smith, –?–, P. Borley, B. Dalziel, Adjutant and Mrs Bourne, W. Bailey, W. Toon, H. Bannister, F. Slater. Seated: P. Hathaway, H. Cox, W. Comley.

Early 1930s. From left, back row: Luke Ford, Jack Rodgers, B. Dutton, Reg Hathaway, W. Porter, P. Hathaway, Ted Smith, P. Bracegirdle, Ben Dytham. Second row: Bert Matkin, Charley Matkin, Billy Matkin, Albert Matkin, Len Smith, Les Hathaway, Reg Keates, Fred Leyfield, W. Record, W. Ecob, C. Button. Third row: W. Aldridge, W. Hathaway, Fred Mortlock, Fred Savage, Herbert Smith, W. Frost, Adjudant and Mrs Swindell, Albert Rodgers, Fred Crawford, George Rodgers, Charlie Jarvis, W. Matkin, Percy Banford. Front row: Bert Leedham, Reg Adams, Eric Rodgers, Joe Smith, Bert Leedham Snr, Charlie Teat (bandmaster), W. Smedley (deputy bandmaster), W. Bailey, Maurice Johnson, Horace Williams, George Toon, Harry Webster, W. Comley.

Salvation Army Band, *c.*1934. Bandmaster: Bert Matkin.

Burton Salvation Army Band at Horninglow Church Garden Party, 1948. From left, back row: Eric Johnson, Joe Smith, Terry Lyness, Bert Matkin, John Matkin, Bill Matkin. Kneeling: Maurice Johnson, David Matkin, Fred Mortlock.

Opposite above: Salvation Army Band, *c.*1948. Bandmaster: Bert Matkin, Deputy: Fred Mortlock.

Opposite below: Presentation of a new set of instruments, 1966. Bandmaster: David Mortlock.

Swadlincote Salvation Army Band

Swadlincote Salvation Army Band, 1935. Bandmaster: Stan Jones.

Swadlincote Salvation Army Band, 1948. Bandmaster: Herbert Ogden.

Swadlincote Salvation Army Band, the March of Witness, *c.*1950.

An open-air service, *c.*1950.

Burton Citadel Young People's Band

The continuing success of Salvation Army bands through the years is mainly due to the teaching and training of junior band members by dedicated bandleaders who work tirelessly to produce young players. One day, these youngsters will take their places in senior bands.

Amongst the most popular and hardworking of the bandleaders in Burton Corps' history is Maurice Johnson, seated behind the bass drum in the photograph below.

Burton Citadel Young Peoples Band, *c*.1950. Band Leader: Maurice Johnson. Left to right, standing: George Selvey, David Mortlock, David Bannister, Stan Bumstead, John Hathaway, Ken Fowler, Trevor Keates. Seated: Roger Matkin, John Matkin, Jeff Squires, Len Russell, Eric Matkin, Bryan Savage, Maurice Johnson, Major Chris Mercer (Corps Officer), Denis Sharp, John Kelsey, Gordon Elson, Michael Savage, John Savage. Standing at the front is Trevor Hathaway, the band drummer.

Ind Coope and Allsopp Silver Band

1950 dawned with the newly formed Ind Coope and Allsopp Silver Band, who practised on Monday and Wednesday evenings and Sunday mornings. The members worked in the brewing industry as drivers, transporters, brewers and bottlers. When one trombonist was asked, 'What do you play?' he replied, 'A paper clip.' The bass drummer, Mr I. Bishop, described the band members as 'a grand bunch' that left you with happy memories.

At this stage, the twenty-four members under their bandmaster, Ken Keates, were only on the first step of the musical stairway to success, but many had musical pedigrees that the area would hear a lot more of before very long.

Between April and August 1953 the band performed in twenty-nine places throughout the Midlands and the North, as well as playing on Lloyds Ground at Burton Albion FC home matches.

Of one concert, Mr I. Bishop wrote:

However, the very best outing which I enjoyed with the band was close to home ground. It was at the 'Bull's Head', Fradley, and we struck off the programme with a Rousing March – Sons of the Brave. Suddenly a large herd of cows cantered to the fence opposite to where we were playing, as if it was for their benefit. They were jockeying for a closer look, pushing each other aside. Then they remained stock still until we finished that piece of music. When we played Finlandia (tranquilamenti) they gently drifted away. They definitely appreciated the music, so that's proof that cowboys play their own guitars to stop the cattle stampeding. I did not know that a good 6/8 march would soothe them – it was a big herd but every one of them stopped grazing and rushed to the fence. It certainly made our day, the Cows and Customer's Concert at the Bull's Head!

Left: Ind Coope and Allsopp, 1950s.

Below: Picture taken at Ind Coope gala and parade. From the left, Bert and Mrs Renton, Jack and Mrs Wilkinson, Don and Mrs Gallimore.

Left: Band sergeant Jack Wilkinson and Des Smith.

Below: Ind Coope Bass Section, 1950.

three

A New
Beginning

The following bands appear in this chapter:

John Taylor School Band
Junior School Bands
Area and County Youth Bands
Burton Music Centre Brass Band
South Derbyshire Youth Brass Band
Ind Coope Burton Brewers Brass Band
Uttoxeter Brass Band
Derwent Brass Band

John Taylor School Band

With the exception of the Salvation Army Young People's Band and the Air Training Corps Band of the 1940s, there were little or no opportunities for young people to learn to play brass instruments as schools only offered recorders and strings.

However, in the early 1960s a handicraft teacher at the John Taylor School in Barton-under-Needwood went to the Newhall Band to play his cornet and realised that one of his pupils also played the cornet. From that moment a few other boys at the school decided to purchase instruments and learn to play with the help of brass teachers, thus the foundations were laid for the eventual development of the John Taylor School Band.

In 1965, Andrew Pennington, the main initial organiser of the John Taylor School Band, was offered a post at Loughborough University, which he accepted. I was then asked to keep the band going, which I agreed to do.

I commenced Monday evening rehearsals as well as lunchtime ones and, with the help of the Parent Teachers Association, purchased a number of instruments and began a beginners group.

In no time at all, with the enthusiastic backing of headmaster Harry Smallwood, the band was a very useful outfit of seventeen players including my eldest son Richard, who by now had joined the John Taylor School. He was already an accomplished player as he was also a member of the Salvation Army Band.

By 1967 the band had grown to twenty-eight players and quite a number of beginners, including three girls, despite the head's warning that they would take over the male members of the band. Although their numbers continued to increase each year, they didn't quite take over, but were eventually on a 35/65 ratio with the boys.

Thanks to Mr Smallwood, I was persuaded to give up my day job with the South Staffordshire Water Authority and go to Alsager Teacher Training College where I eventually received my Teachers Certificate. I returned full time to the John Taylor School and commenced my teaching career in the handicraft department. I was now more able to continue with the band, which had been looked after in my absence by two band colleagues of mine, Mr David Mortlock, bandmaster of the Burton Salvation Army Band, and Mr Harold Hardman, a cornet player and former professional trumpet player.

In 1969 the band was honoured to take part in the NSBBA National Festival.

Thanks to a young bass player in the John Taylor School Band, Peter Friedrichs, whose parents were German but living in Alrewas, near Burton, the suggestion of a band tour of Germany in the summer of 1970 was proposed. Mr Friedrichs duly contacted the Cultural Embassy in Frankfurt and started the ball rolling, arranging accommodation and concerts in that area.

The John Taylor Band, 1966. Left to right: R. Johnson, P. Woodings, I. Evans, K. Thomas, R. Jackson, R. Allsebrook, M. Pheasey, A. Edwards, W. Pheasey, T. Flaherty, B. Lancaster, W. Kerry, S. Showell, C. Allcock, P. Dukes, R. Castle, D. Fearn. Standing are headmaster Harry Smallwood and conductor Eric Johnson.

Before the band left for Germany, however, a telephone call was received from ATV Today in Birmingham, requesting that the band visit the studios the next day for a live television appearance and an interview with myself. Despite the panic and mad rush we made it, and the band opened up the programme with the march *Slaidburn*, conducted by Gwynn Richards, himself a Burtonian. Gwynn later interviewed me and he concluded by saying that, 'A lot of people in Barton-under-Needwood would be very proud today.' The band then played a selection, 'The Best of the Seekers', which was very popular in 1970.

A youth hostel was booked at Wiesbaden for the first three days, with visits and concerts also arranged. The next eleven days were to be spent at the youth hostel at Kronberg, near Frankfurt. This hostel was based on the site of car manufacturer George Opel's private zoo, which proved very interesting to the members of the band, most of whom became particularly attached to George the Hippo!

During our stay at Kronberg a school band from Rendsburg in North Germany joined us at the hostel, and many friendships were struck up between the members of the two bands.

There are many stories regarding that first overseas trip, such as the two girls (nameless, of course) who were crying with homesickness by the time the coach had reached Alrewas, about two miles from home. Secondly, the boy who slept all the way to Canterbury where we stopped at services for the usual. He returned with presents for home, saying that they all spoke good English in there. The band conductor also added to the stories by forgetting to get off the boat on the River Rhine trip after the band had disembarked, and had been carried a further ten miles or so upstream before getting off. Fortunately, his wife found a taxi

Above: The John Taylor Band, 1967. *Below:* In 1968.

The John Taylor Band, 1969.

and set off in the direction the boat took. She met him walking nonchalantly along the riverbank towards them!

The itinerary for that first historic tour commenced on Friday 24 July 1970 at 12.30 a.m. for the 4.30 a.m. crossing from Dover to Ostend. On arrival at Ostend we were horrified to find that the Belgian coach and driver were not there. Half an hour later the driver, George, turned up having gone to the wrong dock. We finally arrived at the Wiesbaden Youth Hostel in the late afternoon.

Sunday was morning rehearsal, afternoon swimming and an evening concert at an old folks' home. On Monday a civic reception was held by the Burgomaster at the Rathaus (town hall), and later we departed for Kronberg. On Tuesday we were treated to a guided tour of Frankfurt Airport, where we gave a concert to the many passengers waiting for their flights. This was followed by lunch in the Stadtwald (city forest) and a concert at Altenheim, another old folks' home. Wednesday began with a trip into Frankfurt and a visit and lunch at the Hans Jugend Haus, followed by a concert at the August Stanz Heim. An evening concert in Königstein, where we shared the platform with the Rendsburg Band, brought to an end another good day. Thursday was a little easier, with a short rehearsal followed by yet another old folks' home concert. It was very pleasing to see members of the band trying to

Richard Johnson, Eric's son.

communicate with the elderly residents. Friday morning included a visit to a natural history museum followed by a trip to the spa town of Bad Orb for an afternoon concert.

On Saturday morning we played at a hypermarket outside Frankfurt and in the afternoon played in a joint concert with the Rendsburg Band at the famous Palmengarten in Frankfurt. One elderly German couple told me that they always came to the band concerts and ours was the best that they had been to. Saturday evening was a concert in the hills at Oberreifenberg, where the concert hall was perched on the edge of a mountain. Needless to say we kept the volume down!

Sunday was spent at the huge open-air swimming pool where we gave an impromptu concert and also swam and relaxed. Monday was an early start for a trip on the River Rhine, which included the Rhine Gorge and the Lorelei, and a visit to the Champagne cellars at

Eltville where the older members were invited to sample the product! Tuesday saw the band playing at the magnificent spa town of Bad Nauheim, where the very wealthy go for the good of their health and no doubt pay for it.

For Wednesday morning we had arranged a football match between Rendsburg and Barton. It was only when the two teams were lined up that we realised that the German team were on average some six inches taller than our team! However, we gave a very good account of ourselves and only lost 2-1. The evening farewell concert was most enjoyable, although some of the girls shed a few tears saying goodbye to their German boyfriends. On Thursday the 6th we said farewell to Kronberg.

The journey home saw one band member smuggling a budgerigar back, hidden in its cage under a truckload of instruments. At the docks, the budgie was chirping merrily away. The Belgian dockers thought that the wheels were in need of oiling and so got out the oilcan without making any difference.

NATIONAL SCHOOL BRASS BAND ASSOCIATION

President: CHARLES GROVES, O.B.E.

Chairman: GEOFFREY BRAND

★

NATIONAL FESTIVAL 1969

OLDBURY TECHNICAL SCHOOL, WARLEY

SATURDAY, 10th MAY, 1969, at 7.0 p.m.

★

Guest Conductor for the Massed Bands

HARRY MORTIMER, O.B.E.

★

SOLO BANDS

MID-HANTS. SCHOOLS' BAND (Hampshire)
ROWLEY REGIS SECONDARY SCHOOL (Warley)
JOHN TAYLOR SCHOOL (Staffordshire)

★

PROGRAMME   -   SIXPENCE

Above: National Festival Programme, 1969.

Right: Sharon Timperley.

Apart from myself as conductor, the staff on that first historic trip included: Mrs L.N. Johnson, Mr H. Friedrich, Miss E. Rees and Mr and Mrs J. McHale. The band consisted of the following girls: R. Fisher, C. Tovey, L. Bourne, H. Kilner, S. Wright, E. Thomas, L. Cox, S. Hunt, V. Fletcher and K. Wright. The boys were: P. Woodings, K. Wildgoose, C. Prince, R. Johnson, I. Evans, P. Silver, A. Kirkland, A. Musto, A. Gee, G. Johnson, T. Thomas, G. Evans, F. Turnbull, J. Carey, R. Mellor, A. Bourne, D. Lucas, M. Mason, S. Williams, P. Friedrich, R. Bullock, I. Wilson, I. Pepperill, G. Hood and L. Carter.

The band continued to give excellent service to Barton and the surrounding district as well as competing in regional and national band contests for the next two or three years. In 1971 and 1972 the band were finalists in the Great Britain Youth Band Championships at Liverpool. In 1973 they were Midland Area winners and finalists at the Fairfield Hall in Croydon during the National Festival of Music for Youth.

The British Youth Brass Band Championships of 1973 were held in Liverpool and were adjudicated by Harry Mortimer, OBE. The John Taylor School Band took part, performing the suite *In Switzerland* by Eric Ball. To add to the demands of the occasion, a torrential downpour occurred as the band played. The event was held in a large marquee and the sound was deafening. Mr Mortimer stopped the band playing until it died down. He commented that the band played with style and character, finishing with a 'well done' at the end.

A very proud moment for all local people was the return of our own Tony Ford from the Commonwealth Games in Christchurch, New Zealand, in 1974. Members of the John Taylor School Band were there to welcome him and celebrate his triumphant return.

Playing 'at home' was always very special too. At one concert, held at the John Taylor High School, the band opened with Eric Osterling's *Bandology*, followed by *I don't know how to love Him* from *Jesus Christ, Superstar*, as well as *Parliament Blues, Brass Band Boogie* and *A Swinging Safari*. Featured soloists were Howard Smith (trombone), Sarah Bennett (flugel horn) and Peter Woodings (cornet). *Finlandia* and *Hootenanny* were followed by several enthusiastic encores and warmly applauded.

Left: Preparing the band for the tour.

Opposite page: Pre-tour rehearsals.

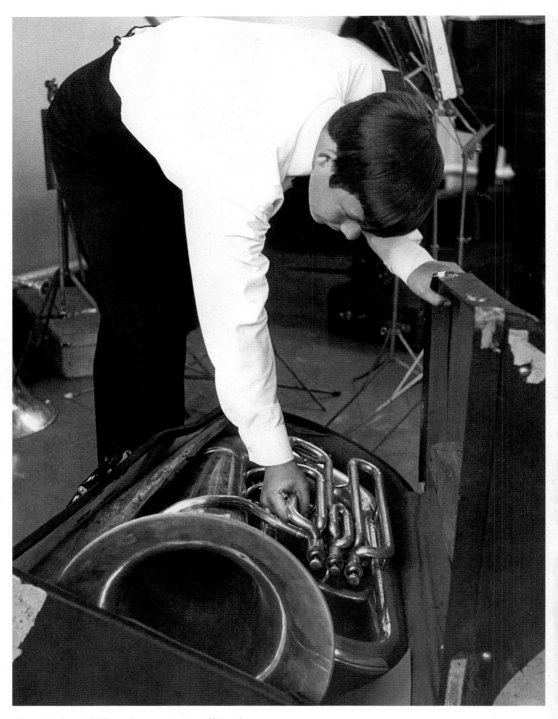

Above: Robert Phillips takes great care of his tuba.

Opposite: Peter Friedrich, whose father Heinz helped to organise the band's 1970 visit to Germany.

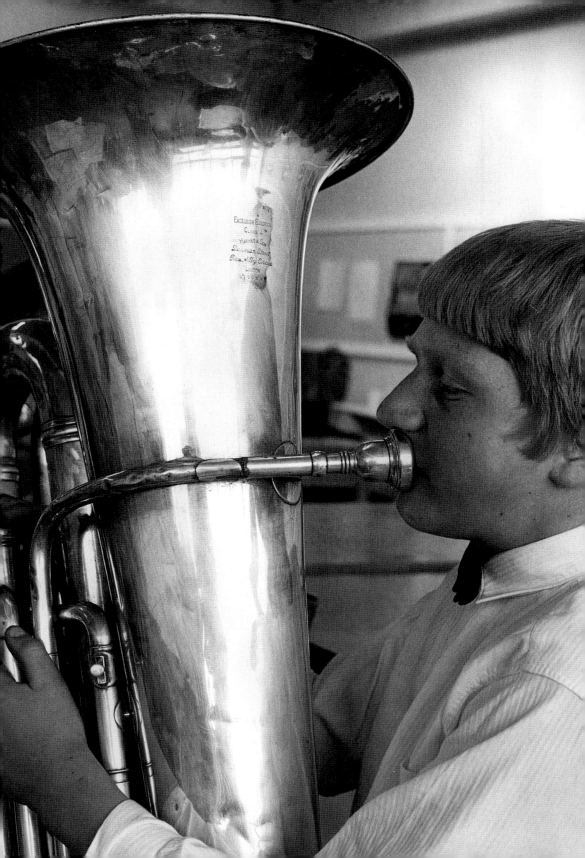

Above: Entertaining the German public.

Left: Lesley Cox, who made a name for herself at the ATV television studios.

Opposite: Spit and polish.

*This page and
following:*
Playing at a
hypermarket
near Frankfurt.

A concert at Barton-under-Needwood Church, compered by television personality Mr Tom Coyne.

A gold medal in the Light Heavyweight weightlifting division for Tony Ford ...

... and, on his return to Branston, near Burton-upon-Trent, the band were there to greet him.

Junior School Bands

1971 saw my departure from teaching at the John Taylor School to taking over the Burton Music Centre from Music Advisor Stuart Gill, although I still continued to train and conduct the John Taylor Band. At that time, brass and woodwind was taught only in senior schools in Burton, and that only in a limited capacity, but now selected junior schools were encouraged to develop their own bands, with youngsters now being taught in lesson time. The main junior schools involved were William Hutson, where Mrs Judith Hambling was the music teacher; Waterside, with Sue Bellamy (now Mrs Beresford); Edge Hill with Mike Ward; and Joseph Clark with Peter Appleby. Schools outside of Burton were still administered by Stafford. The Burton senior schools eventually reaped the benefit of these youngsters.

Below and opposite: Waterside Junior School at Radio Derby, *c.*1973.

Area and County Youth Bands

As players started to develop in Burton, where an orchestra, recorder ensemble and an excellent youth choir were already established, it was decided to commence a wind band and a youth brass band including players from the John Taylor School.

Eventually Burton became a part of the Staffordshire administration, and the peripatetic teaching staff had to be increased to cope with all the extra schools such as Stretton, Rolleston, Tutbury, Branston, Barton and Anslow. Fortunately, we managed to recruit five or six excellent and enthusiastic teachers who carried on the good work started in Burton.

The Burton Brass Band was one of only two in the County of Staffordshire – the other being in Stoke-on-Trent – conducted by Mr Tom Barlow. It too had been taken over by Staffordshire County Music Advisor, Mr John Taylor, decided to put the two bands together and call it the County Band, so each band underwent a name change. Stoke became the North Staffs. Youth Band and Burton became the East Staffs. Youth Band.

In 1977 the County Band visited North Germany under the baton of Mr Taylor, assisted by Tom Barlow and myself. Concerts were given in Bremen, Bremerhaven and towns in the Hartz Mountains, as well as giving a performance on German television. Meanwhile, the Burton-based East Staffs. Band was in big demand locally for concert work, especially at Christmas and for summer fêtes, and quite a few contests were entered, including the Pontin's Easter Contest at Hemsby. Here the band was placed third in the fourth section and was warmly congratulated by Mr Harry Mortimer, who consented to have his photograph taken with the band. The band was also awarded fourth place at the Milton Keynes contest in 1981.

The East Staffs. Band continued with new young players filling the vacancies, and in 1979 visited Holland and Belgium for a ten-day concert tour organised by a Dutch brass band enthusiast named Jurrien De Koning, who lived in Utrecht. The following year, 1980, saw another trip to Holland and Belgium being undertaken due to both the success of the previous year's visit and to the many requests from the people that we played to in 1979.

East Staffordshire Youth Band at the Pontin's Contest, Hemsby 1976, with guest Mr Harry Mortimer.

Left: The Pontin's banner, 1976.

Below: East Staffordshire Youth Band at Burton Music Centre, 1978.

East Staffordshire Youth Band in Burton Memorial Gardens, 1980. Conductor: Maurice Johnson.

Cornet section, 1981.

Burton Music Centre Brass Band

The band continued to visit Europe most years and, in 1984, as a result of Burton's twinning with Lingen in Germany, changed their name from East Staffs. to Burton Music Centre Brass and quickly made friends with Lustige Musikanten of Brogbern, a suburb of Lingen. Very soon arrangements were made for a visit by Burton Music Centre Brass, which proved to be the first of many over the next decade, with the Lustige Musikanten 'Happy Band' visiting Burton on a number of occasions. Many band members from both bands formed lasting relationships and some even went to each other's homes for their holidays.

In 1988 the Burton band visited Austria, where the highlight of the tour was playing in Mozart Platz, Salzburg, in front of Mozart's statue, on a glorious summer afternoon to hundreds of tourists. Unbeknown to either band or conductor, the Deputy Chief Education Officer for Staffordshire was in the throng, and he later wrote to say that it was one of the proudest moments of his life to see and hear a Staffordshire youth band performing so beautifully in Salzburg to so huge a crowd. Further tours have continued, including visits to the Koblenz region, the Rhine Valley and even the youth hostel in Wiesbaden where it all started in 1970.

1982 was a very notable year as far as the young musicians of Burton Music Centre were concerned, for that was the year that Queen Elizabeth decided to pay a visit to her estates in the Burton area. The great day commenced with the arrival of Her Majesty by train at Burton railway station, and it was my privilege and honour to conduct the Music Centre Brass Band in front of the large crowd that had gathered to see the Queen. After the normal introductions to local councillors and dignitaries, the Queen walked over to the band and thanked us all for the welcoming music, which she thoroughly enjoyed.

Burton Music Centre Brass Band, 1982.

My next stop was Tutbury Castle, where the Queen was scheduled to have lunch; my wife and I were privileged to be officially introduced to Her Majesty, who again commented on the quality of the band. During the lunch to which we were invited, the Burton Youth Orchestra played continuously suitable music under the baton of Edward Toon, a former member of the Royal Marines Band, who had played on the Royal Yacht *Britannia* for a number of years. (I wonder if Her Majesty remembered him?)

At the conclusion of the Queen's tour of her royal estates, she finished up at Darley Oaks Farm where Pat Moran had the Burton Youth Wind ready to play during tea. Finally the Queen departed for home, satisfied that her estates and Burton music were in very good shape.

The end of an era took place on 21 June 1992 when Burton Music Centre's final concert took place on home soil in the Town Hall, Burton-on-Trent. Former members of John Taylor School Band, East Staffs. Youth Band and the Music Centre Brass Band lined up along with present-day band musicians. Over one hundred players gathered to perform, conducted by myself. At least as many other players took part, being involved with Burton Youth Orchestra, Burton Senior String Ensemble, Burton Junior Orchestra and the Intermediate Youth Band, as well as the Burton Tuba Quartet. A great richness of players of all ages took part in this unique reunion concert.

1992 saw me take the band to Germany again prior to my retirement from teaching, and once again it was a great success. We gave concerts in Lahnstein, near Koblenz, in Winnington at a wine festival, and in Rudesheim and Koblenz itself. It was enjoyed by all members of the band and staff, especially our drummer, Sandy Malone, who stayed behind at the invitation of the hotel manager, Guido, to play in the hotel each evening for the duration of the school holidays. In fact, I believe that his parents went for a holiday too! The band now has a new conductor who is carrying on the good work and still taking them across the Channel to maintain the *herzliches Abkommen*.

As well as the brass band, Burton Music Centre incorporated a wind band, a youth choir and a jazz orchestra. Burton Youth Jazz Orchestra is the most recently formed group at the Centre and is under the guidance of its creator, music teacher Philip Marshall. Specialising in demanding modern jazz arrangements, the orchestra plays widely at functions and festivals.

Opposite, above: The Queen has a chat to Eddie Toon and Eric Johnson, with Burton Youth Orchestra in the background at Tutbury Castle, 1982.

Opposite, below: This 1989 photograph of the Burton Music Centre Brass Band is taken in front of the bronze statue of the Burton Cooper, which was created in recognition of the town's brewing history. Standing on the left are Eric Johnson, associate conductor Alan Booth, and, behind, Gordon Parker the band chairman. Incidentally, Trevor Standley is not in the barrel waiting for the hammer to descend, he is actually behind it!

Burton Music Centre Brass Band at the William Hutson School, Horninglow, 1989. The William Hutson School and its music teachers, Judith Hambling and Susan Beresford, have been responsible for the development of a great deal of Burton's talented youngsters, many of whom have gone on to play in music groups and to music college, and in some cases even on to the professional scene.

Burton's twin town band, Lustige Musikanten-brogbern.

Above and below: Burton Youth Jazz Orchestra performing at Tutbury Castle, mid–1970s. Leader Philip Marshall.

South Derbyshire Youth Brass Band

The South Derbyshire area has been a well-known centre for brass bands for over a hundred years, having such established bands as the Newhall Band, which made its name in the early 1970s and produced many records and tapes as well as broadcasting nationally on numerous occasions and performing at the Royal Albert Hall. Also the Gresley Band, which is now in its highest ever position in the first section and winning prizes in contests nationwide. The Swadlincote Salvation Army has always maintained a good standard and local bands of the past, including Overseal, John Knowles, Coton, and Swadlincote Town, have all done their part in making South Derbyshire 'Brass Band Territory'.

The success of the John Taylor School Band of Barton-under-Needwood in the 1960s – founded by Arnold Pennington, at that time a teacher at Barton, and continued by myself – inspired the new music teacher at the William Allitt School, Newhall to consider forming a school brass band. This young teacher, Philip King, commenced fundraising with the blessing of the headmaster, Colin White, and the help of an energetic PTA. The John Taylor School Band gave a concert at the William Allitt School to a more than capacity audience. In fact, not only was the hall full, but the corridors as well. Philip then had the valuable assistance of

An early photograph of South Derbyshire Youth Band. Far left is Arnold Pennington, far right is Philip King. Other names we can fill in are John Warnock, Paul Grice, Carol Sibson, Paul Sibson and Steve Perry.

Arnold Pennington, who was able to find a number of reasonably priced instruments, and the William Allitt School Band was on its way.

As the band developed, pupils from neighbouring schools, such as The Pingle and Granville, showed an interest in taking part and, in time, the South Derbyshire Youth Band was formed. A notable driving force with the band in this period was Eric Smith, a former Marine and Salvation Army bandsman. Eric's sound musicianship steered the band through the seventies and early eighties and many young players benefited from his high expectations.

The South Derbyshire Youth Brass Band has undertaken a variety of tours since its inception. Early travels took them to Skegness and Southport and then a link was forged with the town of Bâgé-la-Ville near Mâcon, which resulted in a number of visits to France. Three concert tours of Canada and America resulted in many friendships being formed and the band's reputation being greatly enhanced.

Subsequent conductors have included Paul Smith, Tom Jones, Terry Whittingham, Nick Parrans-Smith and Mervyn Soloman. Each has worked hard with successive generations of youngsters in order for the band to continue giving pleasure to both players and audiences. The band is part of the South Derbyshire Music Centre, which has four bands and three choirs. Although Philip King is now Education Adviser with responsibility for music in Derbyshire, he still actively supports the work of the Youth Band. 'I have been delighted with what the band has achieved over the years,' said Philip. Many players, teachers and parents have dedicated considerable time and energy to ensure that it is handed on to the next generation of young players for them to derive pleasure, as the many others before them have done.

Ind Coope Burton Brewery Brass, 1981-1995

I first had the idea of forming a town band for Burton in 1980 when an article appeared in the *Burton Mail* asking for suggestions to which use of the Burton lottery money could be put. I approached the Mayor of Burton, Cllr Peter Haines, and suggested funding a town band, an idea which he was very keen to pursue. However, his term of office was nearly at an end and he returned to his place of employment, which happened to be Allied Breweries. About this time, a change of name was being considered for the brewery, reverting to the original name of Ind Coope. Peter duly arranged a meeting between the head of the brewery, the publicity officer, Lynette Davidson-Burns, and myself with a view to starting the Ind Coope Burton Brewery Brass for the benefit of the town and giving a musical outlet to the many talented young players who were too old for the youth bands. Money was to be provided for a set of new instruments, a set of uniforms in the brewery livery of green and gold, music stands and £500 towards a library of music. A practice room was made available and the players were invited to meet and commence rehearsals early in 1981.

Out of the original band of twenty-seven players plus myself, twenty-three had been at the Burton Music Centre.

The first public performance was at a garden party at the handicapped centre in Shobnall Street, and this was followed shortly after with a concert at the Ind Coope Club in Belvedere Road, Burton-on-Trent. The first major concert was held at Burton Technical College, when the world-famous cornet player, Mr Jim Shepherd, was the guest soloist.

The band entered the National Brass Band contesting scene in the fourth section and rapidly became the band to be beaten by the other bands as numerous contests were entered, most with excellent results.

This page and opposite: The original players of Ind Coope Burton Brewery Brass Band in 1981.

In 1985 the band spent a most enjoyable week in Valkenburg on the borders of Holland, Belgium and Germany. Numerous concerts were given in all three countries and were very well received.

In the lower photograph on page 87, the soloist David Jackson is playing the xylophone. David is now a professional percussionist who plays for a number of orchestras including The Royal Philharmonic.

One memorable concert was held in the spa town of Bad Neuenahr where the Music Centre Brass had performed two or three years previously, both concerts being held in the famous Kurhaus. In addition the band also played at Eigenbilzen and Herenthout in Belgium as well as Valkenburg in Holland. Needless to say, a Rhine Valley trip was once again a most pleasant experience.

The photograph 'Three Men in a Boat' (one a young lady) on page 89, featured Arthur Ramsdale, Tony Preece and Lesley Barnes. This was taken and used by Burton Town Hall's publicity department for their leisure brochure.

Burton Town Hall featured many great band occasions, especially when we joined forces with the Gresley Old Hall Band and the Newhall Band in a massed band concert numbering some one hundred players, and the numerous occasions when we had the Gresley Male Voice Choir as guests. Possibly the finest night of all was when Peter Skellern was the band's guest and he enthralled everyone with his own particular style of singing and piano playing as well as the three numbers he performed accompanied by the Ind Coope Band. This whole programme was recorded by BBC Radio Derby and broadcast in full on Christmas Day 1990.

The band won many contests and collected a good many trophies and prize money, including the National contests which saw the band promoted from fourth to third and third to second sections over the next few years. Other wins included the Amber Valley competition, the Inter-Breweries Trophy, the Burton Music Festival on more than one occasion and many others from around the country including the 1987 Pontin's Contest at Hemsby.

There have been a great many highlights for the band. Playing at the Royal Albert Hall in the National Brass Band Finals was a great thrill. Although we did not come in the prizes, we still played really well and thoroughly enjoyed the occasion. The band did, however, enter six competitions in 1985 and came first or second in five of them.

Another trip to London took Ind Coope Burton Brewery Brass Band to the studios of CBS, where the band made a recording of *A Glass of Brass*. It was a memorable occasion and the resulting record received excellent comments in more than one national music journal. As well as having certain tracks played occasionally on radio, the band was included on records with other bands, including Manchester CWS and Royal Doulton.

The various open days and fêtes which are held in Burton and district often had a guest celebrity and it was usual to get them to conduct the band. They included Ruth Madoc of *Hi-De-Hi* fame; Windsor Davies, the fearsome sergeant in *It Ain't Half Hot, Mum*, who conducted *Colonel Bogey*, and Keith Chegwin.

Miscellaneous events punctuated the months and years ahead. One of the band's most unusual engagements was to lead a funeral cortège through the High Street in Cheadle in 1989 playing *Colonel Bogey*. This came about as a result of a panic phone call one Wednesday from a firm of solicitors desperately seeking a band for a funeral on the next day, Thursday. The firm claimed that a former police sergeant and latterly publican had died, and that if he did not have a brass band to lead his cortège through Cheadle playing *Colonel Bogey* then all of his estate would go to charity. Naturally, the relatives were panicking and were most relieved to see the band turn up and duly lead the cortège through the town!

Her Worship the Mayor, Mrs Pat Hill, shows the band her robes.

To mark the band's 10th anniversary in 1991 a trip of a lifetime was organised to Orlando, Florida, for six days, playing, meeting fellow musicians and entertaining the USA. The band's personnel on this great occasion were: soprano cornet, Ian Dawn; principal cornet, Patrick McCarthy; solo cornets, Joanna Baker, John Fern, Michael Parker; flugel horn, Fiona Dawn; repiano, Andrew Sharkey; second cornets, Matthew Atkin, Glyn Burroughs; third cornets, Arthur Ramsdale, Sarah Millard; solo horn, Trevor Hazell; first horn Richard Johnson; second horn, Trevor Standley, Lesley Barnes; first baritone, Andrew Hart; second baritone, Karen Bastock; principal euphonium, Peter Broadbent; euphoniums, Glen Satchwell, Martin Kemp; solo trombone, Karen Davies; second trombone, Susan Fern; bass trombone, Paul Hodson-Walker; Eb bass, Martyn Stretton, Carl Richardson; BBb bass, Kate Webster, John Evanson; percussion, Edward Matkin, Philip Marshall, Richard Baxter.

Unfortunately, some of the band members decided to break away and form their own band, which was eventually sponsored by Bass. This band did not last as a brass band for more than two or three years, eventually including woodwind. They are now operating as a twelve-piece called 'Force Ten' under the leadership of Tony Preece. Another small group that also gives good service and comprises many of the former Ind Coope and Music Centre players is called 'Occasional Brass', whilst other players are to be seen in Newhall, Gresley, Uttoxeter and Derwent Brass of Derby bands.

Unfortunately, the Ind Coope Burton Brewery Brass ceased to function in 1995, mainly due to the lack of support caused by the changing circumstances in the ownership and future of the brewery. However, it had been a great period in the brass band history of Burton.

Above and below: Ind Coope Brewery Brass Band entertain the crowds at the football match between Leicester and Derby County, 6 February 1982.

Ind Coope Brewery Brass Band's first overseas tour of Holland and Belgium.

David Jackson on the xylophone.

Three Men in a Boat (one a young lady!).

Opposite, above: A pleasant spot in Holland.

Opposite, below: Waiting for their cue.

Above: After promotion to second section, 1985.

Right: The one that mattered. Third Section Champions, March 1985.

Opposite, above: Massed Bands. Ind Coope, Newhall and Gresley in Burton Town Hall.

Opposite, below: A capacity audience in Burton Town Hall.

The band at Hemsby.

Collecting the trophies at the Amber Valley Contest.

Entertaining in Cooper's Square, Burton-upon-Trent, 1985.

Where the band stayed before playing at the Royal Albert Hall in the National Brass Band Finals.

At the CBS Studios, London, where Ind Coope Brewery Brass made their first record, *A Glass of Brass*.

Opposite: The superb Burton Festival Trophy.

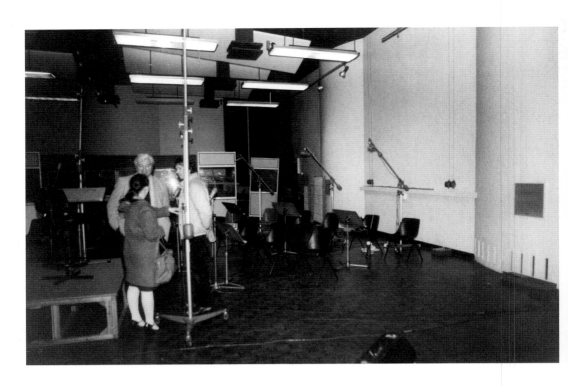

Above: Windsor Davies takes the baton.

Right: Hi-De-Hi! Ruth Madoc, the new M.D.!

Opposite, above: Conductor Eric Johnson with Philip and Mavis Marshall.

Opposite, below: Advertising the band's record with Windsor Davies.

Up, up and away!

Above, and opposite page: The famous Whit Friday March Contests. Dukinfield, 23 May 1986.

Above and below: New planes for Orion Airways are welcomed by Ind Coope Burton Brewery Band.

Concordia Brass Band of the Netherlands welcomed by the Mayor of Burton, Don Furness.

The band in the Ind Coope reception centre, *c.*1987.

Composer of *Staffordshire Way,* Ted Harley, with Ind Coope Band, who performed the piece in Rugeley, 1987.

Above: Ind Coope Band wearing Bass T–shirts at the Epcot Centre.

The band in Busch Gardens, Tampa, Florida, USA.

Guest conductor Erik Osterling, a well-known American composer, conducting his own *Bandology*.

Let's play in the shade.

Opposite: More trophies won by Ind Coope Brewery Brass Band.

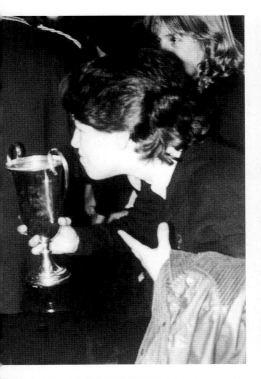

Uttoxeter Town Brass Band

Uttoxeter Town Band was originally formed in the 1930s. It welcomed players from other village bands to share in its music-making, but eventually paused for breath a few years after the Second World War. After a fifty-year pause, it was reformed at the request of Mr Bob Glennan, a local crisp factory owner, and Mr Vernon Cotterill, a local butcher. Both parties had asked me to reform the band and take up the baton as its conductor. Bob Glennan's close friend, Alan Booth, had been on my music centre staff for many years. On Alan's death Bob wished the band to be reformed in his memory, as Alan had been very popular with the young musicians of Uttoxeter.

The Uttoxeter Town Brass Band commenced rehearsing on 27 February 1996 at Bradley House Ex-Servicemen's Club in Bradley Street, Uttoxeter, with about twenty prospective members in attendance. Most could not play a brass instrument. Some had not played for many years, including at least two that had not played for over thirty years. However, a collection of very battered and decrepit instruments gave us the opportunity to start playing. The chosen piece was the hymn tune *Deep Harmony*, which started to sound something like it after three attempts. This hymn tune is still very popular with the band today.

It is very doubtful if any modern band had such lowly beginnings as Uttoxeter, but by June 1996 they gave their first performance at Kingstone village fête. The band's 'uniform' consisted of waistcoats bought off a stallholder in Burton Market!

In the band's first year, they gave over twenty performances in Uttoxeter and the surrounding villages, at all of which they were asked to return the following year.

Uttoxeter Town Brass Band. The very first performance at Kingstone village fête.

St Mary's Church fête, Uttoxeter, 1999.

Uttoxeter Brass Band at Stapenhill Gardens, Burton-upon-Trent, 1999. One of the cornettists, Ken Margerrison, and I last played together at this venue some fifty years before.

The band in new uniforms at Checkley Church Concert, November 2001.

Others heard about the band. Uttoxeter Town Brass Band led the Remembrance Day Parade to St Mary's Church, Uttoxeter and came to play regularly in local churches, schools, clubs, village halls and Uttoxeter Town Hall.

Unfortunately, the rehearsal room at Bradley House became unavailable on our practice evening, Tuesday, so a new venue was sought. The JCB Social Club at nearby Rocester was offered and gratefully accepted. The band continues to rehearse there each Tuesday evening.

From waistcoats, the band is now resplendent in green tunics and has a full set of superb instruments that were formerly the property of the Ind Coope Band of Burton, sadly no more.

The band continues to flourish under the leadership of its new musical director, Carl Richardson, who has played with several bands that I have conducted.

[Carl is the tuba tutor of the Editor – a very small world!]

Derwent Brass

My final band in this compilation of local bands is the Derwent Brass, which is based at Mackworth near Derby. The band's origins go back to the Derby Railway Band. The Davis Derby Band succeeded this until a few years ago, when an amalgamation with a group of mainly ex-Derby Youth Band members called Neville Brass joined forces with some of the Davis Derby Band to form the Derwent Brass.

The band has celebrated its 10th anniversary and can really be proud of its achievements. Commencing in the third section of the brass band contesting league, the band won each section convincingly to reach their present high position in the first section, where, only recently, they came fourth out of the twenty finalists from all Britain at the National Finals held in September 2002 at Torquay.

Derwent Brass has maintained an excellent reputation for the quality and variety of its concert programmes and can always be assured of a return booking wherever it performs. Some of the most memorable concerts have been at Derby Assembly Rooms, Derby Cathedral, Burton Town Hall, the Landau Fort College in Derby and many other places of distinction.

In 2001 the band had as guest soloist Mr Stephen Mead, who is widely held to be the finest euphonium player in the world today. In 2002 the guest soloist was Mr Chris Jeans who, until recently, was principle trombone player with the Black Dyke Mills Band.

Derwent Brass has enjoyed excellent concerts when it has joined forces with Derby Choral Society, with whom they have produced an excellent CD of Christmas music, together with the Gresley Male Voice Choir, Derby Salvation Army Songsters, Derbyshire Constabulary Male Voice Choir, Melbourne Male Voice Choir and many others. The band produced its 10th anniversary CD in 2002 entitled *Celebration*, which is now on sale.

The progress and success of the band can be attributed to the band's musical director, Mr Keith Leonard, who has worked devotedly over the past nine years to develop a quality brass band for Derby and district, and in this he has been ably supported by brass musicians from both Derby and Burton, including myself and at least seven or eight former Ind Coope and Burton Music Centre players.

Derwent Brass in 2003

Derwent Brass is currently enjoying a very successful 2003, having gained promotion to the Championship Section as from January 2004 as a result of their fourth place at the Midland Area Championships in February 2003. The band is thoroughly looking forward to the 2004 contest season when they will be competing with the 'big boys' of the brass band world. Derwent Brass has gained for themselves an enviable reputation as one of the most entertaining concert bands in the Midlands. Keith Leonard, the band's musical director, has to be given credit for developing the band's superb repertoire. 2003 promises to be a bumper year for Derwent Brass, with prestigious concerts in St James's Park, London, in July and at the 'Picnic in the Park' concert at Quarndon Hall.

Above: Derwent Brass, *c.*1993. *Below:* After a contest, *c.*1999.

four

A Tribute to
Eric Johnson

In 1937, eight-year-old Eric turned up for his first lesson in learning to play the euphonium at Burton-on-Trent Salvation Army. After mastering the basics, he was allowed to join the Young People's Band where his father was the conductor. Following tradition in Salvation Army families, Eric progressed to play in the senior band at Burton. When Eric was twenty-one years old he went off to do his national service, during which time he continued his music, playing euphonium in the North Staffs Regimental Band. Most of his time during national service was spent in Trieste, Italy. When Eric returned home to Burton-on-Trent, he took the solo euphonium seat in the Salvation Army Band.

Eric's special musical skills were being recognised and during this period Eric was appointed as the Songster Leader at Burton, while also asked to take on the role of the band secretary. At that time the band needed a new set of instruments and, as the new band secretary, Eric set about the enormous task of fundraising with his typical enthusiasm – and in 1966 a new set of instruments was purchased.

Around 1966, Eric was working as an Inspector for the Water Authority. There was a school band which needed a band trainer and conductor, so when asked, Eric happily accepted this role and took over a small group of brass players from Arnold Pennington. Eric ran the school band, rehearsals, training etc., fitting it all into his lunch hours! We believe this was probably the beginning of brass banding in schools.

Eric found that he enjoyed working with young people and so he completely changed his career when he gave up his job with the Water Authority and went to Teacher Training College. He sold the family house to raise the money to go to college and rented a flat in Barton-under-Needwood for the family whilst he was training. Eric took a full-time teaching job at the John Taylor School in 1968. However he was not teaching music, his first teaching job was as a metalwork teacher. Of course it wasn't long before music inevitably took over, and in 1972 Eric was appointed as the Head of the Burton Music Centre in Bond Street, Burton-on-Trent. There are now of course literally dozens of bands that have talented players amongst their ranks, who were taught by Eric Johnson.

At round about the same time, Eric left the Salvation Army Band and joined the Newhall Band, who were then a Championship Section band. After playing for the Newhall Band for some nine years with many memorable highlights and much success both in this country and in Europe, Eric was still conducting the schools' youth band, members of which were getting somewhat too mature to be called 'youth'. With this in mind, Eric decided that they needed an opportunity to play in an adult band, but apart from the Salvation Army there was no adult band left in Burton. Eric figured that he would put this right and approached the local brewer, Ind Coope, with a view to forming a brand new band in town. As usual, Eric had the magical knack of landing sponsorships from nowhere and the Burton Brewery Brass was formed. A complete new set of instruments was purchased, together with a striking set of green, gold and black uniforms, and it was 'all systems go'. Of course, he had no problems in filling every seat in the band with the more mature youth band players, plus a few experienced players from around the area. Eric hung up his euphonium from serious playing for a short while to progress to new band 'Ind Coope Burton Brewery Brass'. He was its musical director from 1981 through to 1991.

During the Ind Coope period, Eric found it too tempting not to accept an invitation to play principal euphonium with the Royal Doulton Band, who were at this time a very well respected Championship Section band. During his time at Royal Doulton, the musical director (Teddy Gray) retired, and as a direct result the Royal Doulton sponsorship was withdrawn. The band then found itself with no money and no conductor! Whilst some

Burton Youth Brass Band.

would sit and complain, Eric took it upon himself to set off in pursuit of another sponsor, and hence the City of Stoke Band was born.

Following his retirement from work in 1992, Eric joined the then recently formed Derwent Brass, on solo euphonium. His first performance with the band was a Christmas concert at the Derbyshire police headquarters in Ripley. Without doubt most people would have been content at that, but Eric was busy as ever in retirement, being very much in demand as a player and teacher. After an approach was made to him in 1996, he set about forming a new brass band in Uttoxeter with his usual enthusiasm. Only a few months later, instruments had been found, music had been begged and borrowed, a rehearsal room was located, various resting, retired or otherwise available players were found and persuaded to join, and Uttoxeter Band was up and running – with Eric as the musical director.

At the same time he was still occupying the solo euphonium seat in Derwent Brass up until his retirement from active playing in 2002. During those years he was always a totally committed and enthusiastic member of the band and made memorable and invaluable contributions to the band's success. He took part in the band's first National Finals appearance and was regularly featured as a soloist. On his seventieth birthday, Eric was the featured soloist in Derwent's performance at the Buxton Entertainment Contest, playing *Czardas*. His last performance with the band was a concert in the Queen's Hall Derby in June 2002, and doubtless many band and audience members for that occasion will recall his

113

Eric receives the 'This Is Your Life' book to commemorate sixty years banding.

performance of *Blaydon Races*, followed by a moving and faultless rendition of the Welsh air *MyFanwy*.

After retirement from active playing in June 2002, Eric was appointed as the first president of Derwent Brass. During his last few months Eric was still on the phone to their musical director, sorting out players, suggesting music to be played, and was still occasionally attending Friday night rehearsals 'to keep his lip in'!

Eric was one of those wonderful people who would always cheerfully lend a hand to any task that arose, a highly talented and unique bandsman who will be deeply missed by many, many bands people.

five

Personal Tributes

What can we say about the great man that hasn't already been said?! I'm typing this through tears so excuse any mistakes. If God plays brass he'd better be prepared for our Eric. Angels won't be playing harps, they'll be on euphonium. If you keep imagining that you hear *Blaydon Races* with a touch of *How Much is that Doggy*, it'll be our man. They don't make them like that anymore.

Jennifer Marsden (Derwent Brass)

The biggest loss to Derwent Brass in its ten-year history, a small part in his sixty-plus years' contribution to the banding world. He was, is and will always be the biggest personality in the brass band world. Sadly missed but very happily remembered. Farewell Big E.

Chris Clayton (Band Manager, Derwent Brass)

I have much to thank Eric Johnson for. If it were not for him then many of the experiences that I have had would not have been possible. I owe so much to Eric, and many of the places in which I have played I would never have seen if it were not for that great man. He had such a great impact on so many people's lives, and for that reason he will be missed. Thank you Eric for everything you did for me and showed me.

Sarah Kennedy

I have known Eric for about twenty-five years. A man of great stature both physically and spiritually, you always knew when he was there; he had the ability to fill the room in more ways than one. I count myself privileged to have known him and even more privileged to have played with him. Even at the end of his playing career he still had the ability to move me, and probably most of the rest of the audience, to tears. We are all richer for having known Eric and I shall never forget him.

Phil Neville (Ex-Derwent Brass)

I might be young, but even I can see in my time what a massive contribution Eric made to the brass band movement and, more closely to me, Derwent Brass. A fantastic character who will be greatly missed.

Chris Leonard (Derwent Brass)

I just wanted to add to the comments on the big guy, who we'll all miss. A great character and an inspiration to us all; always one for a joke, I'm sure Him upstairs won't mind the Brunhilde wig, musical ties, flashing red noses, etc. etc.

Karen Pitts (Derwent Brass)

Eric and his love for brass bands was very inspiring and you could not help but become addicted yourself, and through my brass band adventures I have visited many places, made many friends and had many pleasurable experiences. He knew how to make music fun. Eric helped to ignite my love of music and I am very grateful to him.

Alison Kennedy

Eric Johnson was one of the warmest and sincerest bandsmen I have come across, and I have never known him to be anything other than cheerful and enthusiastic. A willing and eager bandsman, as well as a talented musician. I am delighted that he was a big part of the last ten years of my musical life and I appreciated his help and advice on so many different aspects. My life is the better for having known Eric – I shall never forget his first rehearsal with

Derwent Brass way back in 1993, or his final performance at Queens Hall in 2002 – we knew we were in the presence of a master.

Keith Leonard (Musical Director, Derwent Brass)

We were very sorry to hear the tragic news about dear Eric. What a smashing chap – you could not wish to meet a more loveable person. An expert at his craft who is going to be sadly missed by all who knew him. We certainly appreciated his playing in the concerts he performed for us, particularly his solos. The 'Friends' have particular memories, since he performed his last concert with us at Queens Hall. His solo performance that night will always be with us. It was a great evening with the presentations being made, and that evening is the way to remember Eric.

Roy Poole (Friends of the Nightingale MacMillan Unit)

I feel privileged to add my tribute to Eric Johnson, who was a very good friend and banding colleague for more than twenty years. He possessed that special quality that enabled him to encourage and motivate players of all levels of ability. Eric was a musician of the highest calibre and a bandsman second to none.

I have many happy memories of my friendship with Eric and Noreen whose selfless support enabled Eric to enjoy a 'life of banding fulfilment'

(*Brass Band World* – November 2001).

The eyesight may be failing but the music is written in the mind.

Burton Music Centre Brass, 2001.

One particular memory, which will always remain with me, is of Christmas Eve 2002. The venue was the 'Beacon', Burton-on-Trent. Eric and a group of his former pupils and friends met to play carols to raise funds for the cancer unit at Burton Hospital, where Eric was receiving treatment. This proved to be Eric's last 'conducting' engagement and despite being in considerable pain (causing him to conduct left-handed) he continued to smile and encourage everyone to give of their best. Afterwards he said, 'that was marvellous, I really enjoyed myself.'

This was just one of many such occasions when Eric brought together players from bands in the Midlands to assist worthy causes. He had tremendous powers of persuasion – you didn't say 'no' to Eric – and even now, several months on, I wouldn't be surprised to receive a phone call from him to help out at a band engagement. He has probably already formed 'The St Peter's Heavenly Brass', but I hope he doesn't ask me to join just yet!

Thank you Eric for your friendship and encouragement.

Dave Bartle (Jaguar Coventry Band)

Eric was my first music teacher when I was nine years old. He started me on the baritone but I soon progressed to the euphonium, his love and now mine. He took me to my first music festival at the Burton Town Hall, which was to become the first of many for me. Over the years we always kept in touch and in June 2002 I was honoured to take over Eric's position as solo euphonium player with Derwent Brass from Derby. I consider it a privilege to have known such a wonderful man who was such an inspiration to many others and me.

Daniel Cheadle

I first entered class music teaching as a pianoforté teacher but soon learned that much fun could be had from brass and woodwind instruments, and the person who was largely responsible for my education in this direction was Eric Johnson. As far as brass instruments were concerned these were a complete enigma. He persuaded me to try his euphonium – his love – which for me proved to be the key that unlocked the door. In the mid–1970s, with the aid of the headmaster and the blessing of Stafford Music Department, the William Hudson School Band was born. He managed to get us instruments, which were loaned to the children. Eric taught these children. As time went by many others bought their own instruments. Between us the band grew to a maximum of sixty-eight band members at one point.

Not only was he the teacher, he was also the Mr Fixit, for as a skilled metalworker, he also mended the instruments and kept them on the road.

Judith Hambling

I feel truly privileged to have had Eric for a father. Eric introduced me to the cornet at the age of six (not that I had a choice) and I have been through countless experiences both under his baton in several bands and playing alongside him in the Newhall Band and latterly the Derwent Brass. As a euphonium player, there have been few ever to match his fabulously pure euphonium sound. The ease of which he played was always a mystery to me and I remember many a contest performance that would have graced the concert halls of the world. In particular, the euphonium solo's from *Le Roi D'Ys* and *Le Carnival Romain* that would always leave you with tears in your eyes. We had so many fabulous musical and fun times together in our banding and he will always be remembered by me not only because of his playing, his joke ties and his larger than life character, but because I was so proud to have him as my Dad.

Graham Johnson

Eric's Funeral – An Occasion in Itself

The funeral took place at the Salvation Army in Burton-on-Trent on Thursday 27 February 2003, and needless to say Eric had arranged for a brass band. This was no ordinary band, but a band of players chosen in the main by Eric himself, covering the many aspects of his musical life; past pupils, Salvation Army friends, colleagues from Derwent Brass etc. Some had travelled many miles to take part and of course none would have missed it. Each and every player felt privileged to be taking part and the band could have been at least doubled with the many more players who would have loved to have taken part. The Salvation Army hall was full to capacity, aisles full of standing congregation, which even stretched behind the band, so many people wished to pay respects.

Eric was, of course, unique, and the arrangements that he had made reminded us of this. Hymns included *Dear Lord and Father of Mankind, How Great Thou Art* and a rousing arrangement of *Thine Be The Glory*. The band were asked to perform Roy Newsome's arrangement of *Deep Harmony* and Peter Graham's arrangement of *Crimond*, and the service concluded with the march *Montreal Citadel*!

A
Memorial Concert
by
Derwent Brass

to celebrate the memory of

Eric Johnson

to be held at the Salvation Army Hall
Moseley Street, Burton on Trent
Saturday June 21st   7:30pm

The band, conducted by Keith Leonard, comprised:

	Position	Band
David Neville	Principal Cornet	Ex-Derwent Brass
Philip Neville	Solo Cornet	Ex-Derwent Brass
Peter Woodings★	Solo Cornet	Newhall
Mick Pattinson★	Solo Cornet	Newhall
Dai Roberts	Soprano Cornet	Derwent Brass
Adrian Beresford★	Repiano Cornet	Derwent Brass
Eddie Toon	Second Cornet	Burton Salvation Army
Gordon Hughes	Second Cornet	Burton Salvation Army
Neville Eden	Third Cornet	Derwent Brass
David Howell★	Third Cornet	Derwent Brass
Nick Henwood★	Third Cornet	Ex-Ind Coope Burton Brewery Brass
Phil McBride★	Flugel Horn	Ex-Desford and Ind Coope Burton Brewery Brass
Brian Savage	Solo Horn	Coventry Salvation Army
Andrea Franke★	First Horn	Uttoxeter Town
Patricia Woodings	Second Horn	Newhall
Melvyn Hale	Second Horn	Uttoxeter Town
Mark Bousie★	Solo Euphonium	Sellers International
Dave Bartle	Euphonium	Jaguar (Coventry)
Daniel Cheadle★	Euphonium	Derwent Brass
Adrian Drewitt	First Baritone	Derwent Brass
Cat Birchall	Second Baritone	Ex-Derwent Brass
Michael Savage	First Trombone	Ex-Enfield Salvation Army
Karen Davies★	Second Trombone	Brackley
Howard Smith	Bass Trombone	Langbaurgh Brass
Carl Richardson★	EEb Bass	Derwent Brass
Ron Banks	EEb Bass	Newhall
Peter Dukes★	EEb Bass	Burton Salvation Army
John Evanson★	BBb Bass	Ex-East Staffs Youth Band
David Lucas★	BBb Bass	Derwent Brass
Sion Hathaway★	Percussion	Derwent Brass
Trevor Hathaway	Percussion	Derwent Brass

★ Eric's former pupils

six

Local Bands Today

A Directory of Local Brass Bands

Burton Music Centre Brass
Musical Director: Adrian Taylor
Practice: William Shrewsbury School, Stretton
Contact: Pam Bale – 01283 815478

Derwent Brass
Musical Director: Kieth Leonard
Practice: Mackworth Church Hall, Friday 7.30 p.m.
Contact: Chris Clayton – 01332 380406

Gresley Old Hall Band
Musical Director: David Hutchinson
Practice: Gresley Old Hall
Contact: Steve Kirk – 01283 760526

Newhall Band
Musical Director: Mark Phillips
Practice: Newhall Labour Club, Tuesday & Friday 8.00 p.m.
Contact: Patrick Marklow – 01283 211588

Salvation Army Band
Musical Director: Edward Toon
Practice: The Citadel, Mosely Street, Tuesday.

Tutbury Band
Musical Director: Malcolm Heywood
Practice: Richard Wakefield School, Saturday 10.00 a.m.
Contact: Mrs B. Harvey – 01283 812091

Uttoxeter Town Band
Musical Director: Carl Richardson
Practice: JCB Social Club, Rocester, Tuesday 7.30 p.m.
Contact: Lynn Weatherer – 01538 754508

School Bands

Abbot Beyne High School
Mill Hill Lane
Winshill
Burton–upon–Trent

De Ferrers Specialist Technology Collage
St Mary's Drive
Horninglow
Burton–upon–Trent

Paget High School
Burton Road
Branston
Burton–upon–Trent

Paulet High School
Stanton Road
Stapenhill
Burton–upon–Trent

Robert Sutton Catholic School
Bluestone Lane
Stapenhill
Burton–upon–Trent

William Hudson Junior School
Harehedge Lane
Horninglow
Burton–upon–Trent

William Shrewsbury School
Church Road
Stretton
Burton–upon–Trent

John Taylor School
Dunstall Road
Barton–under–Needwood

Acknowledgements

My heartfelt thanks go out to the literally hundreds of suppliers of information and photographs, and to David Stacey and the *Burton Mail* for their continued help in publicising this project over the past ten or twelve years. The following list are many those who have helped me and can take some of the credit for my eventual completion of this historical look back into Burton and District's brass band heritage.

Mr Ken Adams; Mr Tony Allen; Mr Harry Bannister; Mr Charles Boyce; Mr Stanley Bumstead; Mr R. Carter; Mr Ron Clay; A. Coates; Mrs Beryl Coates; D.J. Coates; R.J. Coates; Mr John Cox; Mr George Draycott; Mr J.H. (Digger) Draycott; Mr C. Earp; Mr Jim Flatt; Mrs Coral Gould; Mrs Gadsby; Mrs Grantham; Mr Green; Mrs Hardwick; Mrs Barbara Harvey; Mrs Margaret Hazell; Mrs Holdcroft; Mr Bill Hunt; Mr Eric Jowett; Mr George Kerry; Mrs H. Keen; Mr Steve Kirk; Mrs Janet McBride; Mrs Melvyn; Mr Alf Moss; Mr G. Mottram; Mr Arthur Murfin; Mr Ken Phillips; Mrs Pickford; Mrs Powell; Mr Brian George Preston; Mr Jim Ratcliffe; Mr W. (Bill) Roulstone; Mrs Smith; Mr D.B. Stuart; Mr Wilf Sutton; Mr George Swan; Mrs B.N. Taylor; Mr George Thomas; Mrs Tilley; Mr Bill Toplis; Mr George Wheeldon; Mr Wally Wileman; Mr Jack Wilkinson; Mr Frank Wilson; Mr George Wood; Mr Peter Woodings.

My sincere apologies to anyone who I have inadvertently missed off this list, but I sincerely hope that you enjoy our joint efforts in finally producing this compilation.

All photographs and writings are the property of the author except where attributed.

Eric Johnson

First of all I would like to thank Glenys Cooper of Ottakar's without whose help and enthusiasm this book would never have reached publication. Just before Eric died, he made contact with Glenys and she immediately started making enquiries with various publishers with the result that Tempus Publishing agreed to print. Glenys then contacted David Kennedy, who had recently had a book on Tutbury Community Band published. He very kindly agreed to edit Eric's script, which proved to be rather a daunting job, so many, many thanks are due to David and his secretary for all their hard work. There are many more people to whom grateful thanks are due; people who loaned photographs so willingly and those who contributed information of all kind. Many are listed in the Acknowledgements, but I expect there are some who have been missed out, and sincere apologies if you are amongst that number. I have been amazed at the willingness of people over the last ten years (or it may be twelve years) to supply Eric with all sorts of anecdotes etc. So really this book is the result of the reminiscences of the people of the Burton area. Thank you one and all for your help.

Noreen Johnson